The YouTube Marketing Book

How to Build Your Brand and Grow Your Business on the World's 3rd Largest Website

~James Wedmore~

http://www.JamesWedmore.com

Learn the Best Process for Harnessing the Power of YouTube in your Business

The YouTube Marketing Book
How to Build Your Brand and Grow Your Business on the World's 3rd Largest Website

Your 3 Step Process for Harnessing the Power of YouTube in your Business

For general information on other product and services or for technical support, please contact our Customer Care Department with the United States: opportunities@JamesWedmore.com or (949) 264-2685

Do You Have A Registered Copy Of This Book?

Registered members also receive notification about additional training, conference calls, webinars, and video training that I am conducting to help people move their businesses forward. And most importantly, you'll receive updates to this book, free of charge.

Don't miss the opportunity to get all the help that you need in building your successful online business.

Register Your Copy Today:

http://www.YouTubeMarketingBook.com/register

FREE +60 min Youtube Marketing WEBINAR:

Reserve Your spot for this free, special Webinar training as James Wedmore reveals his exact strategies for MASSIVE Traffic & Total Youtube Domination

http://www.YoutubeMarketingBook.com/webinar

Click the Video Player Above!

OR

Click the QR Code Below

Table of Contents

I’m on a mission

Yep, an introvert from Laguna Beach, California has the noble goal of reclaiming YouTube from the onslaught of Cuddly Cat and Rebecca Black Videos. I want to put video back into the hands of large and small business owners who want to use this powerful and free platform to easily and affordably put their companies in front of the eyes of millions of people worldwide.

YouTube has the power of the internet that entrepreneurs have been promised. Think about it, you have the ability to make and market your own online mini-series, produce promotional “commercials”, and create virtual information talk show segments that are available to your customers 24 hours a day.

When you use video the right way, you can meet people, engage them, and build relationships all while you are catching some z’s, dreaming up your next big Online Marketing money maker.

Sounds great, right? But it also sounds like all the other hype that online marketing gurus have been telling you for ages. So, you should be skeptical.

First of all, making money online is not as easy as many would want you to believe. There has been this circulating myth for years that you can just “set it and forget it” and the money will roll into your bank account. No wonder so many brilliant would-be online success stories never get past their first website project!

The truth is this: Making money online, when you do it the right way, can be done; however, you have to be prepared to work at it, be consistent, and use the best marketing methods to let everyone know about your QUALITY product.

Now, I want you to read that last sentence again and notice some key points: Consistent – Marketing – Quality.

The success stories that you hear about are from people that treat their online adventure as a real business, not just a unicorn chasing road to instant riches. You need to have a product (not necessarily your own), you need to understand how to market that product, and the product and information must be of a quality that your customers want.

Don't worry; it's not as scary as it sounds. This book is going to walk you through the exact steps to market your business using video so that your customer will not only find you, but sit up and take notice as they are surfing through hundreds of YouTube videos.

So, Why The Heck Should You Listen to Me?

Before we even begin getting into the meat of video creation and marketing, here are a couple of disclaimers – or maybe I should call them words of encouragement.

I have a film background. I went to film school and had the opportunity to work with cameras, editing equipment, lighting equipment..all the "toys" of the Hollywood elite. Originally, I planned to take this education and go into the world of movies. I loved everything about it, except for one thing.

I'm an entrepreneur. I didn't want a "boss." I wanted to create, but I wanted to create on my own terms. So I decided to take what I learned and use it to explore this whole "online marketing" thing that I was hearing so much about.

So what does this have to do with you? Well, simple. 1) I know something about video. I know what to do, and what not to do. 2) I also know a thing or two about marketing online. 3) You don't have to have a film background to create the killer videos that I'm going to show you in this book!

In fact, all you need are a few basic skills.

It took me 4 years and thousands of dollars to learn what I'm going to teach you in this valuable little book. You see, I went the traditional education route where I first learned all the theory, tricks and tips in order to get to the core of the most important steps for creating killer video that you can use to market your business online.

It's not going to take you that long...and you can rest easy that you won't need a loan!

So here is a Big Tip: Don't get too hung up on the technical side of creating video.

What You Can Expect from me, and What I Expect From You

This book is all about techniques that work. You're not going to find a lot of "fluff"; leave that up to the bunnies. We are going to cover what you need to know and how you need to implement what you learn to excel your business online using the power of video and YouTube.

You will learn:

- How to Create Killer Videos without Killing Yourself
- How to Implement a Video Strategy that Builds Consistency and Reputation
- The Key to Online Marketing Success (which has NOTHING to do with Video)

In return, I expect you to:

- Take Action!

You cannot market your business on theory. You cannot succeed in any business on theory. Success is the result of Action. Not just any action, but the kind that is strategically set into motion using the best tools, technology, and techniques available right now.

And, my friends, that is Video and YouTube!

Ready, Set…Take Action!

Creating Killer Videos Without Killing Yourself

The first thing you must grasp is the BIG picture. Trust me, you can learn all the information about file sizes, formatting and how to upload to YouTube from anybody. What I'm going to give you in this section are the essentials for creating videos that engage your audience, drive traffic to your sites, and ultimately convert that traffic into sales.

After all – at the end of the day it's about conversions, right? That's what pays the bills, keeps the lights on, and keeps you humming along toward the goals that you have for your business.

Yes, there are a lot of very, very cool things that you can do and create when you start implementing video into your business. And, it can go way beyond YouTube…but that's a story for another day!

But like I told you in the beginning, you don't need a film degree, you don't need to be a super star, and you don't even need to do all the necessary work yourself to be successful with marketing online using Video and YouTube. So, bottom line, don't panic.

We are going to walk through this step by step. I'm going to literally take you by the hand and walk you through the most important steps for effectively using Video in your business.

Alrighty then…let's get into the 7 Steps for Creating Killer Video!

7 Essential Elements Your Video MUST Have

There is no way to "create" a viral video. You really don't control that process. What you *can* do is create a great video that will engage your audience. Then, you can implement some marketing strategies to push your video out to the masses. "Viral" then falls into the hands of the people. But there is still no way to "create" a viral video.

Those that have tried have failed…often miserably.

So what can you do to give your video the best chance of an eager reception? You can have a plan. You don't want to just throw something together and hope that it sticks. By adding a few of the basic elements that are included in every successful video, you have a better chance at getting the kind of attention you hope for. If enough people share it, then, and only then, will your video become viral.

Just like a car has 4 wheels, an engine and headlights – your video must have these critical elements in order for them to run properly.

Intro or Video Bumper

This can be great for boosting credibility. A "bumper" is the industry term that refers to a short clip, usually an animated logo, that people see before watching your video. It's very short –like 5 seconds – and is the video equivalent to a business card. Not everyone uses them, but it's something to consider. You can even use them just at the end of the video.

Here is one example of how you can effectively use a bumper. Let's say that every week you do a short video that answers a question that your audience may have. You bumper could "brand" your "Quick Question Thursday" or "FAQ Friday."

Another example is if you are doing a series of videos that will help your customers build their skills. The bumper could be "Mastering XXX"

The effect is similar to the intro of your favorite television show. But don't worry, there is no need to spend a lot of money to get a bumper created. Once again, you can look to a place like Craigslist. Here are some other sources:

- Fivver.com (where you can get things done for $5)
- www.DoneForYouVideo.com (my friend Lou Bortone – more money, but when you're ready it's a great source to consider)
- And finally, check your search engine for "sizzle reels" or "video bumpers"

Proper Titles

This may sound a little obvious, but it's important to mention.

Your title and thumbnail photo give people an idea about what they can expect from watching your video. If you don't deliver on that promise, you're going to be eaten alive and lose credibility.

You can have the worst video in the world but the title better say, "This is the worst video in the world" (which is actually pretty catchy). The bottom line is that there must be congruency between your title and the content of the video.

YouTube viewers go through titles in much the same way someone would scan a newspaper or magazine headline to determine what they are going to devote their time to. So yes, you want something that is going to pop out and grab their attention, but also something that is SEO friendly and conveys the meaning of the video. That's a lot to think about, right?

Yes – and you should think about it. Your title is the "curb appeal." Make it great and people are going to want to open the door and see what's inside. Make it crappy or leave it up to chance, and they will drive right by.

So, if you're not a star copywriter, how can you create an engaging, catchy title? The best answer is to take time to review videos that get a lot of views. Choose videos from your niche and in other niches and really try to see what seems to be working in the title. There is no crime in following examples of what works, and then adding your own genius to it.

For Example: I typed in the keyword “flat tummy” into the YouTube search box and then sorted the videos by the number of views. I want to look at the top 10 results to see what popped up.

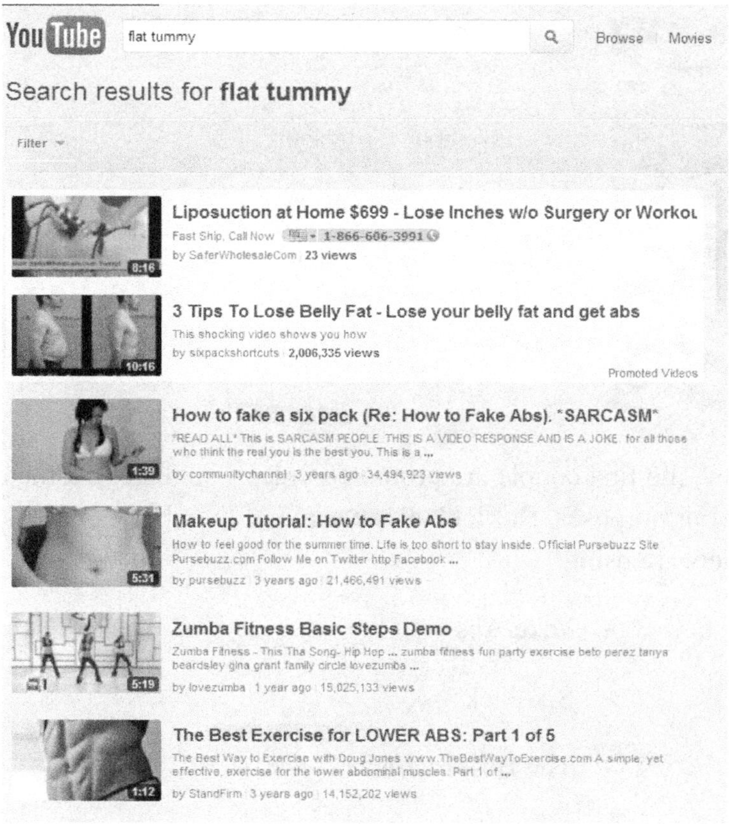

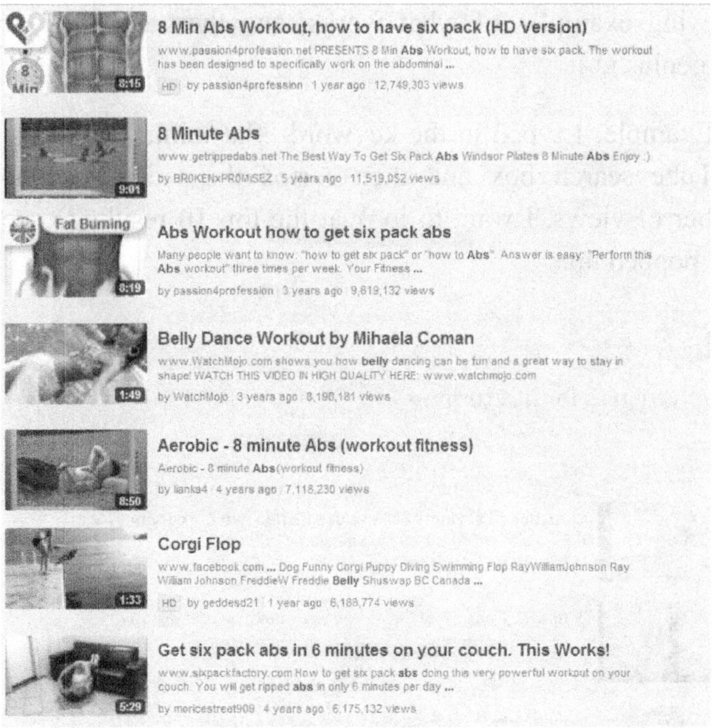

Now, the first couple are promoted videos, so disregard them for our purposes. But look at the some of the phrases that the others are using:

- Fake Abs
- Six Pack
- The Best Exercise
- 8 minute Abs
- Six pack abs in 6 minutes

It seems that the benefit of getting results in as little time as possible is an appealing idea for people working on their tummy! And, the phrase "six pack" is something that will catch people's attention.

Another tip is to log in to YouTube and look at all the most popular videos in your category as well as others. To get the most accurate results, be sure that you are logged out of your YouTube account and any other Google accounts, otherwise your results will be geared towards other things you've searched for or watched (personalized search).

Call to Action

This one is not so obvious which is exactly why many great YouTube videos don't result in traffic back to the entrepreneur's site. Remember, views do not put money in your bank account. Traffic that is then converted to sales is what will help your business to grow!

Ok, so you're getting people to watch your videos – now what? Even if you have the most entertaining and informative video ever made, you can't expect people to visit your website unless you ASK them to. That's what's called a "Call to Action" or CTA.

So what, exactly should you be asking them to do? Some examples are:

- Subscribe to your channel
- "Like" your video
- Watch the next video in a series
- Click on a Link
- Boycott a product
- Join your community
- Vote for something

You can do this in a couple of ways.

First you can verbally ask them. For example you can say, "This is what I want you to do right now. Click on the link below and it will take you to a page where you can get a free video series on XYZ."

Another way is to add some annotations to your video that tell the viewer what action they should take. These annotations can be added directly in the YouTube platform, or you can put them in through the editing software that you're using.

There are other little tricks as well, but these are two of the most basic ones. The most important thing to remember is to ASK.

Keep it Short

I think it's a lot to ask of someone for eight, nine or ten minutes of their time to watch a video, especially if it's their first time visiting your YouTube channel. That's why I recommend keeping your videos short, like 2-3 minutes in length. This is also why it's important to give your viewers a reason to watch your video within the first 10 seconds.

This doesn't mean that you have to do a crazy stunt; it simply means that you need to give them an idea of what your video is about and what benefit they will receive by taking the time to watch the video.

Watching any video is an investment in time. If your viewer was looking in a newspaper or magazine, they would most likely scan the headlines and then maybe read the first paragraph or two of a story that captured their attention.

This same concept comes into play when you do Video Marketing. Something about your video will catch a person's eye. This could be the video's title or the thumbnail picture. They click on it and then quickly listen to the first few seconds to decide if there is anything in the video that is of value for them.

If not, they will move on to the next video they find. However, if you say something that matches what they are looking for or piques their interest then they will stick around for just a little bit longer to see if you deliver on your promise and give them what they need.

Now at this point a question that I often get asked from my <u>**Video Traffic Academy**</u> students and coaching clients is: What if I have something of great value to say and it takes way more than 3 minutes to cover?

That's a great question! The first thing I would suggest is figuring out if it makes sense to cut the content into a series of videos. If there is a way to lead your viewer from one video to the next with a continuity of valuable content on a certain subject, then you keep them "hungry for more" and willing and eager to consume the next video.

If the content is great and provides value, you will get views from people that are interested in the topic. There is no "rule" against creating a longer video. Just be aware that in most cases you will find that the shorter, the better.

Sometimes, you can use the longer video to place on your blog and use a shorter teaser video on your YouTube channel to lead them back to your site. Just be certain that the longer video does, in fact, have great content and not too much fluff. Don't fall in love with the video for the sake of the video. Fall in love with the valuable content and edit out anything that seems to ramble. When you start to ramble, the attention of your viewer will wander.

Editing

Which leads us right into editing.

I believe the more cuts, the better. A "cut" is a transitioning from one scene or image to another. This keeps your viewer engaged and helps create a pace for the story that you're trying to tell.

I suggest watching a few videos to see which ones hold your attention and why? If the pacing is too slow, you're much more likely to move onto the next. If the tone of the voice is not engaging, then your viewer will have a hard time staying engaged even if the content is interesting.

But what if your video is simply an educational piece with you talking into the camera?

That's a great question and one that I get asked a lot. There is nothing wrong with these types of videos. I do them myself in fact. My advice here is to get to your point very quickly. Even if your video is 3 minutes long, make sure that you give something of value within the first 15-30 seconds. So, before you even get to editing your video, consider editing down your content to adequately cover your key points.

You see, people can sense when you're trying to drag something out. And if this is what you're doing, then you risk annoying people. With a click of their mouse they can express their frustrations by clicking out of your video and onto your competitors.

The opposite is also true. If you tell your viewers what they can expect right off the bat, and then you deliver what you promised, they will be amazed! And your reward will be that they may click through to your site, join your community, or simply watch the next video that you have available.

YouTube has some editing options right on their site, but I like to do all my editing before I upload the video, so I'm not really that familiar with their options. If you are looking for a quick way to simply trim the edges and then add some **annotations**, then the YouTube option may be all you need.

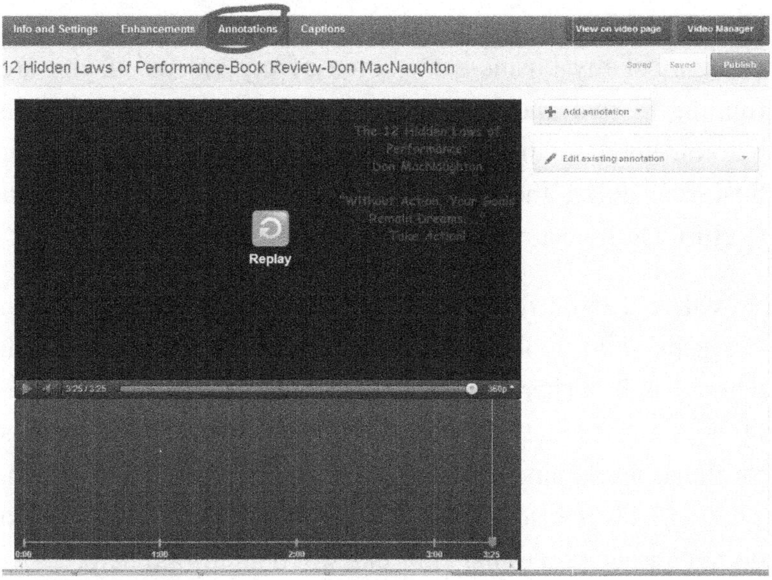

If you're a Mac user, like me, then a really great editing software is Final Cut Pro; if you're on a PC then you can use a simple program like iMovie or Movie Maker. Another option for PC and also now for the Mac is Camtasia.

In fact, you can make videos without even owning a camera by using slides created in PowerPoint and then recording and editing your presentation through Camtasia or Screenflow.

The final option is for YOU to avoid editing! Now, before you get worried, I'm not suggesting that you avoid editing altogether and set out raw footage, bloopers and all, for everyone to see (and laugh at!). But, there is no hard and fast rule that says that you are the one that has to do the work. You can hire someone to take your video, your series of clips, or your "vision" and turn it into a great video for your YouTube marketing.

And…it doesn't have to cost a fortune!

Even though I have a film background, and I have the skills and knowledge to edit my videos, I still choose to outsource this part of my business for some of my videos. If you are running a "real" business, then it just makes sense to get a helping hand so that you can work on other areas of your business, doing the activities that give you the best ROI (Return On Investment – of time in this case).

So where do you find this help? Well, you can put an ad on Craigslist and look for a film student or someone with editing skills. There are also very talented people living in other countries that can help with your project. Some sources to check are: Elance.com, Freelancer.com, and Odesk.com. There are other resources for Outsourcing, but the ones listed do not charge you to list your classified ad to find help.

I suggest that you pay an agreed amount per video. With something like video editing, you don't want to set it up on an hourly base. For example, for a video that is 2-3 minutes long you may pay $40 for the completed video. If the amount of editing you are looking for is not very complex, you could even pay less than that.

Be Engaging!

What the heck does this really mean?

For some people, talking into a camera is really tough, especially if you are filming alone with just you, a tripod, and a little red light on your camera that says you are "on." As a result, the video tends to be a little dry, a little boring and really doesn't project the enthusiasm and passion that you have for the subject you are speaking about.

Know this: Being on camera zaps about 50% of your energy. So that means that you have to exaggerate that energy when you hit the record button in order for your voice, tone, and actions to come alive to anybody who watches the video.

You don't have to go over the top, unless that's your personality and matches what you are talking about. But you do need to create your video presentation as if you are interacting with one person. Think about it. When someone finds your video on YouTube and chooses to watch it, chances are they are alone. So if you talk into the camera as if you are talking to your ideal customer, that one person, then you will have a great opportunity to draw them into your world.

This means that you need to be a little intimate, like you're talking to a friend at a coffee shop. Your vocabulary should include words like "I", "you" and "us."

You have a very good chance of losing that connection if you present the video as if you are teaching in a large auditorium to a roomful of faceless, nameless, students that you don't know or want to know! The vocabulary for this type of video would include words like "everyone" or "one" (such as "one would believe that…") as if you are talking in the third person. This will make you seem aloof and not very approachable.

Think of the T.V. show, The Office. As the story unfolds, the actors tell the viewer (you) secrets and directly look at the camera. Everytime they do that you are drawn into their life, into their minds. They are completely transparent which allows you to SHARE the experience with them.

And that my friend, is the reason that video is so effective when you use it to market you and your business! Your viewers get to share the experience with you. You get the opportunity to take them on a journey with you. They are your roadie, your confidant, and your friend.

You may be hearing a lot these days about Relationship Marketing. With the exploding popularity of Social Media and the fact that content is shared very easily among millions of regular, everyday people, the power of great video, great content, and great relationships can be the tipping point in your business.

Want More? Watch this to Learn How to Make Videos Online MORE ENGAGING:

Link: http://www.jameswedmore.com/make-videos-online-more-engaging-do-these-2-things

Take a Stand - Be Bold

When you start doing video, the only thing that you're really concerned about is getting the darn thing to look halfway decent, making sure you don't have anything gross stuck in your teeth, and then getting it uploaded to YouTube so that you can finally see the results of all your sweating, stuttering and gnashing of teeth!

Then, as you get more comfortable with being in front of the camera (and, trust me, you will!), you start to become more concise and effective in delivering your message. You start to gain some notoriety and a fan base and you will develop a sort of "mini-celebrity" status among your niche. That's a very cool thing!

And then it's going to happen…you are going to encounter your first critic. For no apparent reason someone is going to take the time out of their "very busy" life to send you a scalding message, or make a not-so-nice remark, and you may feel personally attacked for simply trying to make a living!

Why did they find it necessary to point out that gap in your teeth, or your "annoying" laugh, or the fact that you wore the same shirt in two of your videos…really?

Online, we have a word for these people: Haters.

Yes, you'll also have tons of adoring fans but the more successful you become and the more visible you become, then the more likely you are to attract critics – the constructive kind as well as the just plain mean kind.

It's really strange because no one will have a problem with you as long as you're not making progress, but the moment you begin to gain momentum you'll soon have strangers and friends doubting that you got there on your own merit. It's a sad truth, but take it as a sign of success.

So, why do I mention this?

Because, the possibility of attracting some "haters" should not make you afraid to take a stand. You can't please everyone and if you plan on being successful then trying to please everyone should not be a part of your business plan.

One of my favorite quotes comes from something Bill Cosby once said:

"I don't know the Key to Success, but the Key to Failure is to trying to please everybody."

Now, before you start to think that this is just about ego, think of this concept in terms of business principles.

When you create a product or service, will you be more successful if you develop it for a very specific long tail niche market, or will you be more successful if you try to make it for "everyone?"

When you do the very basic steps of Keyword Research, do you have more success when you use a more specific, targeted keyword phrase (like "How to train your German Shepard") or when you use a more general keyword (like "dogs")?

Another way to look at it is with something David Brinkley said:

"A successful man is one who can lay a firm foundation with the bricks others have thrown at him."

So don't be afraid to take a stand in your videos, and don't try to please everyone. Not only will this cause you to lose sleep, but it will cause you to lose views! That's right. Who wants to see someone who has nothing unique or controversial to say?

You don't have to be controversial just to be controversial. But if you can add value and a great viewpoint to a discussion in your niche that goes against what everyone else is saying, then do it! Have your facts straight so you can be confident and ready for any response and engagement that may come for your audience – both the fans and the "haters."

There is actually a word for this technique in marketing. It's called polarizing. What you are doing is creating an "us" versus "them" feel to your videos. When you take a stand that is going against the status quo, and you appear to be willing to risk it all to say exactly what must be said, your viewers will love you for it

This isn't lying. This isn't a trick. You still must be authentic and really believe in what you're saying otherwise it will backfire on you. I used this strategy when I worked on a marketing campaign in the dating niche. We went out there and challenged other experts, saying that anyone who's telling you that you have to manipulate women and play mind games doesn't have a clue about how to get women. We held firm to a platform that dating was not a "Game."

The results? Either people agreed or disagreed with us. But either way, we got tons of views and lots of feedback. People responded in a very passionate way. We had a very lively debate and the final result was that we were Engaging. (Remember that last step we talked about?).

I'm confident that if we had simply done a "me-too" video that was saying the same thing about dating that everyone else was saying that we would not have received the same response…or have gotten the kind of recognition that we did. That video was great for that moment, but also kept many of the viewers coming back for more.

What are Some Ways to Stand Out?

At this point, you may be asking yourself how you can accomplish this same thing with your niche. Start by asking yourself the following questions:

- What hot buttons are there in your niche that you can challenge?

- What are some of the common videos being shown in your niche and how can you put a new spin on them?

- Look at the videos that have a lot of comments on them. What are they commenting about? If there's a disagreement taking place, what is it about? Can you create a video response to this that would make people stand up and take notice?

That's how you've got to be thinking. You need to do a little investigating to see what issues your viewers care about. Then, get involved in the conversation through your video.

Case Study: Will it Blend?

Let's take a look at an example from the "Will It Blend" series created by Blendtec. For those that aren't familiar with these popular YouTube videos, I suggest taking some time to watch a few of these presentations as just one model that works for a "Demonstrable" video that "Engages" the audience by putting a spin on sometimes popular ideas/products/subjects. The Blendtec people are able to successfully show off their product, which is a high quality blender, by drawing in viewers with other iconic and interesting subjects.

The basic premise is this: Every week they create a new video where they blend something crazy like an iPhone or a credit card. They even blended a Just Beiber CD which generated over 300,000 views (and counting).

The videos are not only engaging, but they are also search friendly as they relate to a current event or trend. By piggy-backing on a popular topic, they have an opportunity to pull in more viewers. Who would have ever thought that a video about a blender could be tied into an iPhone or Justin Beiber CD?

Are you starting to get some ideas? Even if a “hot” topic is not directly related to your niche, there may be a way to put a spin on it and get some attention.

Here are some other examples:

- You are a life coach and match up some of your advice as it relates to the recent topic of hoarding;

- You are a marketing coach and analyze a recent political speech to point out some of the marketing techniques used;

- The latest pop rock boy band hits the top of the charts and as a coach you can talk about how to work as a team.

FEAR of Being in Front of the Camera

OK, so let's talk about that 2 ton gorilla in the room – your FEAR of being in front of the camera.

For those that don't struggle with this fear I think that you can still benefit from the tips I'm about to share, so stick around.

First of all, you don't have to be in front of the camera. There are other techniques that you can use to create great, engaging videos without ever putting your mug in front of a camera lens!

- Screen capture and/or slides
- Search Narrative
- Public Domain Video
- Other people

So let's talk about these.

Screen capture and/or slides

You're going to need some software for this type of video. If you're on a PC, then Camtasia and PowerPoint are the ones of choice. I believe that the newest version of PowerPoint allows you to record your slide presentation so if you have that version, you may not need Camtasia. If you're on a Mac (which is what I use) you can use ScreenFlow. Both are great programs and get the job done.

In these videos, you will be the voice but your screen capture / PowerPoint slides will be the face. And yes, you can Outsource the creation of your slides and even the voice if you would like. If so, then you take your idea and concept and draft up a copy of what you want to talk about in your video presentation, and then send it off to a video editor to work some magic.

Here are some great examples of this type of video:

http://www.youtube.com/watch?v=gza8dvN8Hkc&feature=g-vrec&context=G2d16fc9RVAAAAAAAADA

Source:
http://www.youtube.com/watch?v=LqvuhWczgrg&feature=related

There's also another option to create videos without getting in front of the camera and that's through a site called Animoto.com.

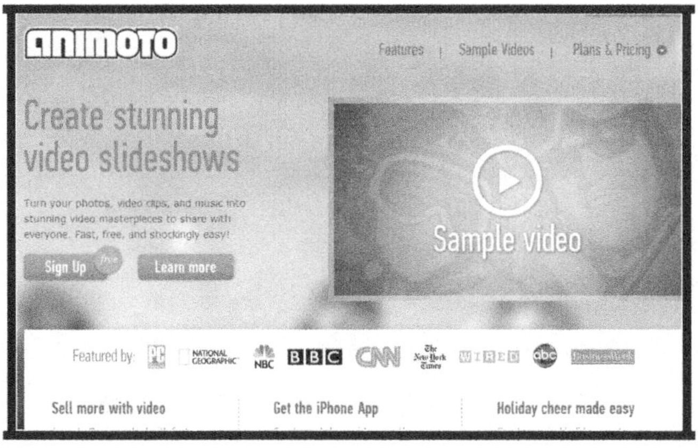

You can take a series of pictures and create a collage type video. It's a simple 1-2-3 process in which you upload your

photos and add text if you want, choose music from their own catalog of choices, choose a theme, and then let their software arrange everything. Bada-bing, bada-boom, it spits out a cool little video. There is a free version and a paid version, so if this type of video would work with your niche, check it out!

Finally, I've got a recommendation for those who would like to dig a little deeper into the world of Camtasia. You can learn all the step by step details of video editing, where to get the text, where to get the images, how to set everything up in PowerPoint, make smooth transitions, add music…the whole nine yards.

Lon Naylor is a friend of mine. He's a great marketer, a very smart guy and he's been doing this forever. You can start with a free account and access to Camtasia and go through Lon's stuff where he will show you how to do all the very cool techniques that you need to learn to make killer videos.

Search Narrative

Here's a resource that very few people know about: www.YouTube.com/create

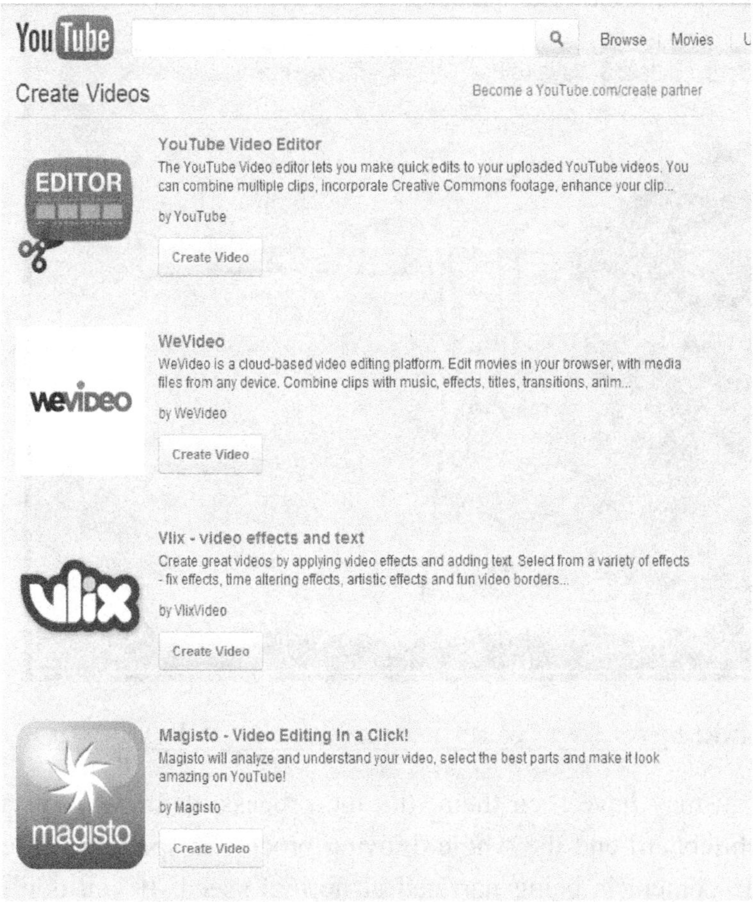

They have recently added to the editing choices offered on the site. You can get some cool little videos done for free, with a small upgrade, or by getting credits. Some include animations so if you have some time and the desire, go

through the various options and find out if there is something there that will work for you!

The "new kid on the block" for video production without getting in front of the camera is what is known as "Scribe" videos or "Scribble" videos:

Link: **http://www.youtube.com/watch?v=y3BOJnyi9zQ**

You may have seen them. It's the process of drawing on a whiteboard and the whole drawing process is sped up while the content is being narrated at normal speed. If you don't draw, don't worry. With a little bit of searching through your search engine, you can find an individual or company that offers the service to produce these videos.

Public Domain Video

I learned about this resource from a good friend and brilliant marketing guy, Tony Laidig.

(http://publicdomainblog.com/) Tony is better known as "The Public Domain Expert" and he showed me how we can legally use tons of Public Domain Video to add a little flair to our video marketing strategy. This is great for some of the "B-roll" footage that you can edit into your videos.

Public domain is copyrighted material in which the copyright has expired and ownership has reverted to the public, so anyone can use it. I don't know exactly how it works, but copyrighted material only stays in copyright status for so long and then it's dumped into the public domain. What that means for us marketers is that there are thousands of videos, movies, commercials and written content that were created in the 1930's and 1940's (and some even more recent) that are now up for grabs. You can download them, edit them, and upload them for your use onto YouTube.

One of the websites that you can go to and find these videos is http://www.Archive.org. There are plenty more out there, but this site will give you a good start. My suggestion is to take an old commercial, tweak it, and put a modern day spin on it with modern music.

WARNING: Going through all the old footage is addicting! You can literally spend hours without even realizing it.

Other People's Talent

One technique you can use is to use other people in your videos. A good format is through an interview where you ask the questions and have experts in your field or in related fields answer those questions. Some people may worry that this will ruin their credibility if they are not the ones fielding those questions.

That's a good question, and the answer lies in the power of curation.

If you are the one that is gathering all the best information that is relevant to your audience, then you will become that "go to" person. They will come to rely on you to sort through the massive amounts of information on the internet and bring them only the cream of the crop which saves them time.

As for monetization, if your experts have products that they have created you can have an affiliate relationship and receive a portion of any proceeds from sales that may result from that interview. This is the exact business strategy that is behind JV Webinars. There is no reason to believe that it wouldn't work for your expert interviews.

Another option is to have video testimonials from your clients. If they have purchased your product and LOVE it, then give them the opportunity to share their experience with others through video. A good testimonial video will give actual benefits that they received, or actual results they had when they used the information in your product.

Rather than just say, “This is a great product, buy it.” Coach them a little bit so their testimonial sounds more like this: “Before I used this product, I was struggling to get even a dozen views on my videos. Now that I purchased **Video Traffic Academy**, I am consistently getting hundreds of views on my videos each week. And, the best part is that more and more of those views are turning into paying orders! When James Wedmore talks about YouTube as being a social media platform that uses the power of Relationship Marketing, he’s not kidding. I now fully understand that developing a relationship with my customers using video is a lot easier than any other marketing method out there…”

A Final Note on Fear

These are just a few of the options you can use if you are a little camera shy yet still want to produce great videos. Even though I personally enjoy being in front of the camera, I still make videos using the methods talked about above, especially when I'm using video for affiliate marketing.

All that really matters is that you deliver on what the title of your video says it's going to be about. Let me encourage you to at least give it a shot and get in front of the camera yourself. I've had a lot of clients and students of mine overcome this exact same fear, so I KNOW that you can too!

Here are some steps you can take to get comfortable in front of the camera:

1. Practice and mistakes will HELP you. If even professional movie stars have bloopers and "deleted scenes" then how can any of us expect to be perfect? Don't expect to get it right the first time or expect to like everything you see No one has to see what you shoot. You can delete it right away if you'd like but keep in mind that you're probably going to be your toughest critic. It may take as little as 3 takes to get comfortable and many more in the beginning. It's curious, but often "Take 3" ends up being the best!

2. Talk Slow. Talking fast will make your words get ahead of your thoughts and make you sound nervous…this will MAKE you nervous.

3. Get a second opinion. Even if you think your video sucked, get a second pair of eyes on it. A close friend will be able to give you pointers and encouragement. This may be the first time that you've seen yourself talk, but your friend, the one that has been watching you talk for years, has a better idea of what you normally look like when you have a conversation. So, that kind of makes them an expert on what you should look like, don't you agree?

4. Focus on the content. As long as you focus on how important your message is, you'll distract yourself from the fact there is a camera recording you! The only people who have anything to fear on video are those that are inauthentic, lying, or cheating. So keep your focus on your content and forget about the camera. Some people will go so far as to tape a picture of their ideal customer on the camera and then speak to them directly. This helps visualize who you're teaching and who you're talking to. If it's authentic – your passion on the subject will come through.

5. Spontaneity. You're at the beach, on a hike, in the mountains, or waiting in a restaurant for your food to arrive. This is the perfect time to get out your camera and record a video. These kinds of videos are great – they add authenticity to you and your videos because they are unfolding in reality. Don't believe me? Just look at the popularity of "reality TV" and you can see how engaged people become. Folks love to get a little peek into your life.

6. Energy Management. You must be a little louder and a little more animated than you are in a normal setting. It's interesting, but the camera seems to zap your energy so it's vital that you show expression, and add some life to your voice otherwise you will come across as boring.

So, try to film at the best time of day, when your energy is at its peak. For some, this is in the morning while others will be late at night. Just find your best time to shoot and then do it!

All of this may feel a little weird at first, but it will make your videos come to life. Remember, even if the video is meant to be informational, this is entertainment!

The Nitty Gritty Details

Which Camera Should I Use?

The best camera to use is the one that you're most comfortable using.

I use my iPhone half the time now. If you've got the iPhone and it has a video camera you can shoot your video and instantly have it uploaded to YouTube in seconds. You can even edit the video right on your phone before uploading! How much easier can that get?

Another way to record your videos is through your computer or with the use of a webcam. I have a client and friend who has been very successful with his online business and video marketing by using this method. In fact, very often the recordings are done at a coffee shop with all the hustle, bustle and sounds of clanking of coffee cups in the background. When it comes to "Relationship Marketing" how more real can you get than if you are actually having that cup of coffee with the person on the other end of the lens? Brilliant!

If you are looking for a great camera to purchase, then you are in luck because with the advances in technology you can get something for less than $200.

The Kodak Zi8 – The quality of your audio is one of the most important things to consider when it comes to the overall quality of your video. The Kodak Zi8 gives you the opportunity to have a wired or wireless mic which enables you to get crystal clear audio. And, you can purchase a great lavilier mic for as little as $20.

Kodak Playsport HD – I recently picked up this camera for a trip I took to Catalina Island. It's waterproof which is cool, but it doesn't have the audio jack for external audio. It is, however, very social media friendly which is an awesome feature. This means that you can automatically upload your videos to YouTube.

The Importance of Sound

Can I make a suggestion?

Invest in wireless microphones. Sony sells a great wireless set for $500, but you can also find a decent pair for $50. Check thes eout :

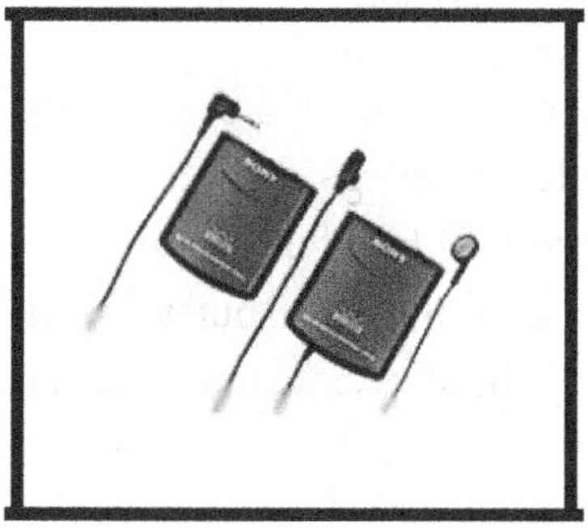

If you can get these, that's great. But remember that your camera must have an audio jack in order for them to work. Your viewer will forgive you if the visual aspect of your video is a little off, but they will show less mercy if the audio is bad. No matter how good your content may be, if they have to struggle to hear it, or if you are competing with loud or distracting back noise, then they will move on.

Editing

The goal of your videos is to drive home one point and then keep your viewers wanting more. If you answer everything in one long video, then there is no reason for them to ever visit you again, right?

That's why you want to keep your video short and concise.

If you film something that's demonstrable make sure you film it from the best angle possible as well as from a variety of points of view. The "best" angle will be your establishing shot which will be the majority of your video, but you can use the additional angles as other points of view that you can quickly cut to.

Cooking shows are usually very good at this, but you can easily use the concept with any niche video. Check out this example for Cooking With Dog:

Link: http://www.youtube.com/watch?v=PeUHy0A1GF0

Even when you don't have the advanced editing technique of cutting and filming from various angles, you can still great results by using very easy annotations and close-ups. Most editing software will allow you to do this lickety-split!

One of the best examples of great content, and great editing using cuts and annotations comes from my good friend, Marie Forleo – check her out!

Link:
http://www.youtube.com/user/marieforleo?feature=watch

Editing Software

iMovie for Mac is super easy and FREE! (yay!)

It comes with templates, transitions and title sequences – all the cool stuff you'll need to create a professional looking video. The other very cool feature is that is comes with a ton of stock music to add to your video.

If you are on a PC, you can use Windows Movie Maker. And, as I mentioned earlier, you can also test out the features on Camtasia for editing your "in-the-face" videos as well as those created without your image on camera.

Tips on Tracks

When you're editing, it's best to have separate video and audio tracks because once you start playing around with the editing software you'll quickly realize you can do some clever stuff with both video and audio. So, keeping them separate is important.

And remember, if you don't want to learn to edit at all – hire someone else to do it for you. You can give them a vision of what you want, or show them examples of other videos that you find engaging and then allow them to create something for you.

Lighting

Remember how I said that sound was the most important thing? Well, next on that list would be lighting. Before you go out and buy a professional lighting kit, I'm going to save you a ton of money and give you a quick list of what to buy.

There is a great lighting kit that you can find on Amazon. Just type "cowboy lighting." There are a couple of options, but the one that I personally use and have set up in my office is the one with 3 lights. You place one light just a few feet above your head, then the other two point toward you at a little bit of an angle so that you don't get any funky shadows. The whole setup is portable, so you can take it with you as well. This is so convenient to have set up and ready to go when you film:

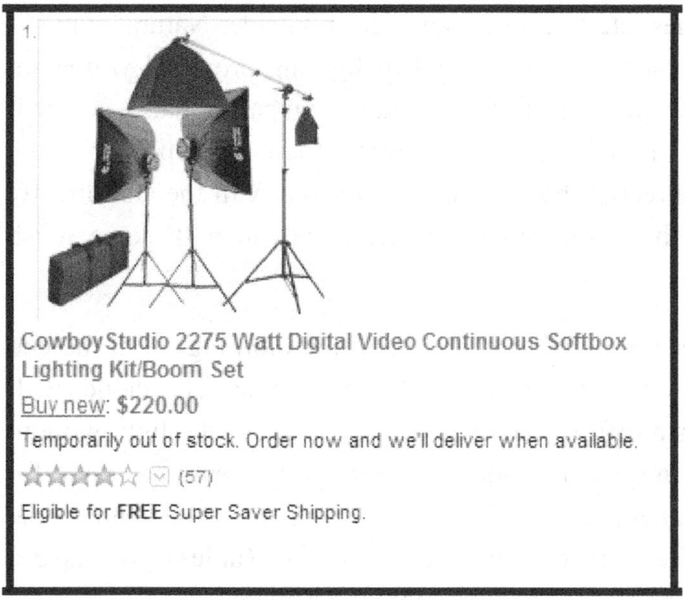

Another type of lighting can be purchased at your hardware store. The basic clip on or clamp lights that you may see in a workshop are inexpensive and can do the job.

But remember, there is another great and free source of lighting that is available to most people year-round (with exception of some locations in the Polar Regions!). That's the sun!

Don't hesitate to shoot your videos outside. Natural sunlight offers you the perfect blend of lighting provided you shoot the video at the right time of day. Typically, that means that you will avoid the hours between 10am and 2pm when the sun is directly above you. If you shoot with the sun directly above, then you will most likely end up with some harsh shadows.

A better time of day would be in the morning, or at the end of day, or even when it's cloudy outside. The clouds will work as a diffuser and will evenly disperse the light without casting any harsh shadows. When you invest in a tripod for your camera, you will have a greater ability to film in the right direction to capture the best shot (unless you have a camera-person available to hold the camera).

Music

If you are going to use music in your video, the biggest tip is to be sure that it's not so loud that your content is competing with the tunes. This is especially important if you're talking.

The second thing is to be sure that you have the rights to use the music in your video. This is easier than it sounds since there are so many sources to pick up royalty free music.

Music is important, but it's not a must. Not all videos need it. But if you want it, there are plenty of places to go:

- www.SoundBakery.com
- www.SonicFirePro.com
- www.Pawn5.com

And, there are tons more sites available. All you need to do is Google "Royalty Free Music" and you can pay anywhere from $10-$30 for a music track that's top of the line quality.

Be cognizant about using music. Maybe you want to brand yourself with a certain little trailer sizzle song to put at the beginning and end of your videos, which I totally support.

Creating a Video Strategy that Builds Your Reputation

I have a little bit of a confession to make. Some people call me a "Video Expert", but I'm not! Actually, there are a lot of times when I actually get stumped on those "What" kinda questions that people ask me like "What camera should I use", "What format should I upload in", and the like.

Yet, I'm still seeing HUGE results using video in my business!

So how can this be possible? How can a film student not know everything there is to know about video and still be successful with Video Marketing?

First, technology moves way too fast to keep up to date with all the latest and greatest video making "toys" while still working to run a successful online business. And, while it's good to be aware of changes in the technology, I find that finding something that works and using it fully is also a good way to go. The reason that I'm successful with Video is:

Because I FOCUS on the HOW!

In other words, I focus on the STRATEGY of using video. I'm actually an Online Strategist who focuses on how to effectively incorporate video into my marketing (not just teach people how to edit a video). SHHH! Don't tell anyone!

So, if you want to get real results with your videos, then you need to put a strategy in place. You have to have an idea about HOW you are going to use video to drive traffic, build your brand, and increase your online exposure. You have to give some thought to HOW you are going to turn visitors into leads and then into customers easily and effectively using Video.

Answer that question, and you have a Video Marketing Strategy!

In the courses and trainings that I offer, such as Lights-Camera-Expert, I go in-depth into all those places within your marketing strategy that you can use video to see increased results:

- Video Traffic (YouTube)
- Video Conversions (Squeeze Pages & Sales Pages with Video)
- Content Creation (Video Training)
- And Much, Much More!

You might be offering a physical product or a service, it really doesn't matter. You can use the power of video to fully engage your customers and get the kind of online business success that you had really hoped to achieve when you started your business.

In this book, we are covering just one of those areas which is the Traffic that you can get through YouTube. I have thousands of happy students in the **Video Traffic Academy** course that will eagerly agree with the potential of using YouTube in your business!

How to Create Video Production Strategy

I have a white board in my office, one of those old school 8' x 4' white boards where I have listed all the future videos and blog posts that I'm going to create. This helps me create a "big picture" sort of editorial calendar for what I want to cover.

When you create a "Big Picture", this does a couple of things: 1) It allows you time to get a game plan in place so that you're not constantly stressing out about what in the heck you're going to talk about in your next video 2) It allows you to develop some great content that your customers are interested in hearing 3) It takes that "task" out of your brain and then frees up brain space so that you can become even more creative!

So, whether you use a whiteboard, smart phone or iPad – I suggest writing out a video series. For best results, write out the next 6 videos you're going to make. You can then upload them once per week so that you have a CONSISTENT flow of content for the next month and a half!

Now, you're probably asking yourself how you can figure out what to shoot in your videos!

A good method is to start with your keywords. Most people in the internet marketing space understand the importance of using keywords for SEO, so I'm not going to go into that here. What I would suggest is that you make what I call a "shot list" of 30 keywords that you want to target for your niche. That shot list becomes your video list and you will create 1 video for each of those keywords. When you've gone through the list, you can either make another video for each of the keywords, or create a new list of keywords to work from.

Other areas that you can look at for video content are:

Past blog posts and articles that you've already written. The written content is already there, so why not just get it on camera so that you can use this additional marketing platform in your business?

Look at blog posts and videos from your competitors. Can you create videos with an opposing view? Or, was there some missing information that you can fill in with your own style and point of view?

Check out Yahoo! Answers. People are asking questions, and this is a great place to find out what people want to know. If they have a question related to your niche that you can answer, turn on the camera and answer it!

Check out Niche Forums. Just like with the resource above, your audience may be hanging out and asking questions in a forum. Find out what the conversations are and then contribute via your YouTube video.

Check out Social Media. Yep, that's Twitter, Facebook, LinkedIn...wherever your target audience is hanging out. Again, these are ongoing conversations that may spark an idea for a great video.

Your job is simply this: Uncover what people want to know more about and then produce the answers in a video.

Get Into a Video Rhythm

I've learned that if I pick one day as my filming day, where I batch together at least 3 videos, and as many as 6, I not only leverage my time, but I also create the momentum which puts me in a rhythm, gets me excited, and motivates me to easily move to the next video.

Think of it. If you're uploading 4 videos a month and shooting all 4 in the same day, you'll quickly get ahead instead of falling behind. This momentum will begin to translate into other areas of your life as you begin to get 1-2 months ahead of yourself in content creation. This pace also allows you to have the time to watch trends and current events and then be able to add additional videos as it makes sense. These could be your spontaneous or "breaking news" kind of videos without taking away from your series.

I mentioned the use of an editorial calendar. You don't have to get all formal and you shouldn't even overthink the concept. However, as a publisher of content it works well to follow what industry leaders in the world of offline magazines have done for years. If you have an idea of the topics you want to cover, you can plan out the best time of year to distribute that information, or the best way to present your series so there's some cohesion.

Then, with that out of the way, you've got time to get creative, have fun, and be spontaneous!

So pick a day each month, or each week, and then shoot as many videos as you can. If you're worried that it's going to look like you shot all your videos in one sitting and your thumbnails will be all the same, then simply change your clothes and move the camera to a different location.

This method for shooting your video also goes for editing your videos. Pick a day where you can sit down and edit a handful of videos in a single sitting. It's sorta like an assembly line, and can be very efficient.

Batching together similar tasks in all areas of your online business will make everything much easier. Multi-tasking may sound great in theory, but in practice studies have shown that it is very inefficient as your attention is divided.

Even if you are outsourcing your editing to a site like www.OnlineJobs.ph or www.Odesk.com be sure that you are doing it on a set schedule. This helps your VA's and editors be more efficient as well.

Tips for Outsourcing Video Editing

There are some great online tools that you can use to transfer large files, such as your raw video footage, to your Outsourcer. The one that I use is www.dropbox.com. They have a free and a paid version, and which one you use will depend upon the volume of video your doing. Start with the free version. You can "drop" your unedited footage files into a folder that's shared with your Outsourcer and then they can easily pick it up on their end.

The most important thing to remember is that you're crystal clear about what you're looking for. Don't expect your editor to create a masterpiece without any instruction. They are simply being hired to follow your vision. If, on the other hand, you'd like an editor to use their creative expertise to tell a story and create a visual masterpiece then I suggest posting an ad in Craigslist or through a local college, but be prepared to pay $30-$50 an hour.

Once you get a response to your ad, I recommend that you try out a few editors to see which one works best as well as which one you get along with. This is a creative partnership so it's important that you and your editor have a good vibe.

Make sure you keep track of how long it takes for you to shoot a film, submit to your editor, and then finally upload to YouTube. This will allow you to get an idea of how long it takes to get something turned around which in turn will allow you to properly plan your time. Once you have this process down you can then have the confidence to know exactly when you can upload new content. Trust me, this kind of confidence and rhythm is what will set you apart in this business!

Key to Online Marketing Success

Finally, once you have the basics of creating your videos and have established a consistent routine of getting them produced, you still need to create and implement a system to get those videos seen all across the internet so that people can find you. This is often called distribution and syndication…and it can be exhausting.

In fact, if you take a look at all the steps just involved with creating a video – from the initial keyword research, to the content, to the creation of the video, to the filming of the video, and then the editing, you may be starting to wonder how any **one person** can possibly get anything done in their business!

And the answer is: They Can't!

Wait a second, you may be wondering. "You mean that I just read through this whole book and NOW you're telling me that it can't be done?"

Well, not exactly. It can be done, of course. People are doing it all the time. I do it all the time. But, I don't do it alone!

There is absolutely no way in the world that I could get the kind of results I'm getting and still have a life if I tried to go solo-preneur. Yes, that may sound all romantic and noble in theory, but in reality going at it alone just doesn't work…not online anyhow.

So, the key to online marketing success as I have found is with outsourcing.

We've already talked a little bit about outsourcing the editing process of your videos. This makes complete sense to most people because it's a sort of specialized task and we are somewhat used to hiring people when we don't have the training to do something. It's much like hiring a dentist or a hairdresser.

But what about those things that we can do? Is it okay to hire someone to do those kinds of things? Stuff like uploading the videos, posting them on our Facebook channel, or providing links in all the social bookmarking sites. Then, what about the keyword research, writing the content, finding images for our PowerPoint slides, and even managing the content on our blogs. If we have the skill to do that ourselves, is it "cheating" to hire someone else to do it?

Heck no!

You can literally hire out almost all areas of your business and keep the parts that you love the most – the parts that energize you – for yourself. It's what all CEO's do as they sit at the head of their businesses and steer it in the direction that they want it to go. Remember, you are a CEO. And, the faster you let other people use their talents and time to work in your business, the faster **you** will be able to work on your business and manage its growth.

That IS the Internet Lifestyle!

For more information on Outsourcing your business: www.6FigureOutsourcingSecrets.com

Take Action!

Alright. I've just given you all the tools to start shooting killer videos for your business. I've done my part just as promised; now it's your turn.

- Do a little Keyword Research
- Create your Shot List
- Draft up your Content
- Dust of the Camera
- Create a PowerPoint Presentation
- Lights, Camera, Action
- Do some simple Edits
- Upload the video to YouTube
- "Push" your video out to the web
- And then do it all again!

I love using video marketing as a primary tool for my online business. And…bottom line is that it works.

There is so much more that I can show you as you continue to use video for your online business. Be sure to do all of the following to get the most Success with YouTube Marketing:

Register a copy of this book to continue to get all the Exclusive benefits that my subscribers get at: www.JamesWedmore.com

Check out my other Video Products which can help you with growing your business to its full potential:

www.VideoTrafficAcademy.com

www.LightsCameraExpert.com/next-class

www.6FigureOutsourcingSecrets.com

www.VideoSalesMagic.com

And of course, if you have any questions, comments, or success stories using video I would love to hear from you:

James@JamesWedmore.com

Congratulations on your commitment to reading through this book and taking action to get the success you crave in your Online Business. Until next time…

James Wedmore

p.s. here's a free gift for you!

FREE +60 min Youtube Marketing WEBINAR:

Reserve Your spot for this free, special Webinar training as James Wedmore reveals his exact strategies for MASSIVE Traffic & Total Youtube Domination

http://www.YoutubeMarketingBook.com/webinar

Click the Video Player Above!

OR

Click the QR Code Below

Made in the USA
Monee, IL
04 March 2025

13470182R00046